THE GOOD ROLLERBLADER

and other sketches

Instant drama for schools and churches

Jon Webster

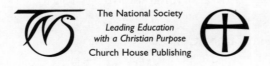

The National Society
*Leading Education
with a Christian Purpose*
Church House Publishing

National Society/Church House Publishing
Church House
Great Smith Street
London SW1P 3NZ

ISBN 0 7151 4944 X

Published 2000 by National Society Enterprises Ltd

Illustrations by Christina Forde and Julian Smith
Cover design by Julian Smith
Printed in England by Halstan & Co. Ltd

CONTENTS

INTRODUCTION

After twenty-seven years as a primary school teacher in England, I know just what it's like to be faced with presenting a class assembly in front of the whole school, and probably the parents as well. You might even call me a veteran!

I've always enjoyed using drama on these fraught occasions. Performing gives me a real buzz, but as a teacher I know that it's vital to get the class involved in the story-telling process. This is why I began writing the scripts in this book.

At one school where I spent seven years, the children gave anyone leading an assembly a hard time. It was a battle to hold their attention – whether you were a teacher or a visitor. Some visitors used drama but, due to enthusiasm and lack of experience, they left the children over-excited. Before anything like normal service could be resumed in the classroom, the children had to be brought down to earth. This created some unease among the staff.

So I began to search for a formula that would enable teachers to use drama in a controlled way, and these plays are the result, the product of much thought and experiment. It's said that trial and error is the best way to learn, but this is not always very cost-effective. The scripts below have been written to help you bypass the blood, sweat and tears.

Some plays retell traditional stories. Others attempt to translate the parables into a modern setting. Hence the good Samaritan has become the good rollerblader helping an old lady who has been mugged by a gang of hooligans. A busy headteacher (we all know one), a hard-pressed school nurse and an off-duty lollipop lady pass her by, each with a plausible excuse. The cool, and unlikely, hero soon strikes up a rapport with the victim and all's well that ends well. I'm afraid the church is commonly perceived as fuddy-duddy and out of touch. This is one small effort on my part to redress the balance.

The church used drama for religious education in the Middle Ages at a time when few ordinary people could read the Bible – it may even have been St Francis himself who organized the first nativity play. Then drama fell out of favour and it was not really until the 1970s that it began to be used again, with the work of the Riding Lights Theatre Company at St Michael-le-Belfry in York. Their seminal sketch, the Good Punk Rocker, inspired my own interest in the medium, along with the rock musical, *Godspell*.

Most of these sketches feature a 'chorus' (All) and very short parts for the characters. The need for props is minimal. The scripts can be acted by the children or used for puppetry. Whichever medium you use, you might like to have your group or class sitting in a straight line behind the puppetry/acting space, facing the audience. I've found this arrangement useful for a variety of reasons:

☆   the cast all feel involved and can see the action without turning round;

☆   the cast can join in with the actions and say the lines labelled 'All' while facing the audience;

☆ individual puppeteers/actors can step forward and immediately be in position to perform on the puppetry/acting space.

I hope these sketches will provide a stimulus for reflection and discussion on the moral and spiritual issues they raise. They have even been used for guided reading during literacy hour with a Year 4 class I taught last year. We discussed the main features of the text: dialogue, stage directions, scene setting. Then the children made their first attempts at script writing and puppet plays, based on the skills they were beginning to develop.

So have a go! Try the scripts out with your own class, and have fun! Education should have its lighter side.

Do email me at puppets@education8.freeserve.co.uk for any extra help you need, or you can write to me at 22 Hobart Drive, Stapleford, Nottingham, NG9 8PX.

Jon Webster

P.S. If you enjoy *The Good Rollerblader*, why not try my other book of sketches, *The Rich Pop Star*, also available from Church House Publishing.

MODERN PARABLES

OUT OF PLAY

Bible reference
Matthew 25.14-30

Theme
The parable of the talents: using the gifts God has given us

Cast
Narrator
Miss Evans (Teacher)
Terry Smith
TV presenter
Michelle Davies
Mick Wilson
Kevin Hill
Six or more football team members (All)

Props
Footballs for Terry, Michelle and Kevin, glass for Mick, newspaper,
envelope with ticket, whistle for Miss Evans

There is no need to signal scene changes – the words of this play should indicate the location of the action.

The chorus (All) need to chant like a football crowd and join in with the actors' mimes.

(All sing Match of the Day *tune and sway as if holding scarves*.)

Narrator	Every football team needs a good manager – well, at least a good games teacher! Our story begins at a school not too different from yours.

(All shouting, arguing.)

Narrator	Quiet! Somehow Miss Evans had to turn this shambles into a team. She began to teach them how to work as a team.
Teacher	Mark him!

(All point.)

Narrator	She gave up her lunch break to get the team fit.
All	1-2, 1-2. (All do exercises.)
Narrator	At the end of the season, they won the district cup.
All	We are the champions! (All hold up arms.) Three cheers for Miss Evans. (All give three cheers.)
Narrator	Then the team left school.
All	All the best, Miss. (All wave.)
Teacher	I just hope they'll go on playing soccer.
All	Bye, Miss! (All wave.)
Narrator	But Miss Evans never forgot her cup-winning team. She was always reading in the paper about Terry Smith, the Rovers' striker.

(Enter Terry.)

All	Hat trick for Smith. Read all about it!
Narrator	Terry was never out of the headlines.
All	One Terry Smith, there's only one Terry Smith!

(*All sing to tune of* Guantanamera.)

All	Goal!
Narrator	Terry was soon rich and famous.
TV presenter	This is your Life, Terry Smith!
Narrator	But he never forgot his old teacher.

(*All sing* This is your Life *tune, de-da-de-da*.)

TV presenter	Come in, Miss Evans, the games teacher who put Terry on the road to the top!
Terry	Thanks for everything, Miss!
Narrator	Miss Evans knew that Dave Roberts was the captain of the local team, struggling at the bottom of the third division.
All	Come on, the Albion!
Narrator	But one day an envelope dropped through her letter-box. It was from Dave.
All	(*Chanting*) Albion! Albion!
Narrator	Dave hadn't forgotten all he'd learned from Miss Evans and he was sending her a ticket for the big cup tie against . . .
All	Manchester United! United! United!
Narrator	She was thrilled with Dave's letter – and the ticket! But there was another top player from her championship team. It was Michelle Davies.

(*Enter Michelle.*)

	Michelle was now the captain of the England Ladies' team and played for Doncaster Belles.
Teacher	Come on, England!
All	(*Chanting*) England – England's Number One!
Narrator	And there was always Mick Wilson – he played for a local side on a muddy old pitch down by the canal.

(*Enter Mick.*)

All	(*Miming*) Squelch! Squelch!
Narrator	Every week Miss Evans went down to cheer Mick's side.
Teacher	Come on, you Reds! Sort them out, Mick!
Narrator	Mick still got a kick out of the game.
All	Ooooh! (*Mime getting a painful kick*.)
Narrator	The teacher was so glad that they were still using the skills she had given them. But where was Kevin Hill? One day she met him in a pub.

(*Enter Kevin.*)

	He didn't look very fit.
Kevin	(*Holding glass*) Aye up, Miss Evans.
Narrator	She asked him if he was still playing.
Kevin	No chance!
Narrator	He said he just watched football on TV. Then he asked if she could get him a ticket for the United game.

All	What a cheek!
Narrator	Miss Evans was furious.
Teacher	What a waste!
Narrator	And she walked off, disappointed that he was not using his skills like the others.

Reflection

God has given all of us special gifts to use and share. When we use and share these gifts, like Terry, Dave, Michelle and Mick, the world is a better, happier place. But if we selfishly waste these gifts, like Kevin, who gave up football as soon as he left school, the world is a sadder place, and, eventually, we will lose our gifts.

THE GOOD ROLLERBLADER

Bible reference
Luke 10.25-37

Theme
The parable of the good Samaritan: kindness, sharing God's love with everyone

Cast
Narrator
Mrs Green
Nurse Goodbody
Mrs Smith, the lollipop lady
Mrs Brown, the headteacher
Gary the rollerblader
Mob of four or more

Props
Handbag, nurse's hat, lollipop(!), register, rollerblades

The chorus (*All*) play a big part in this sketch, especially in their conversation with the narrator at the end. Keep the action crisp and snappy.

(*Enter Mrs Green, walking slowly.*)

Narrator	Hey, look! There's Mrs Green. Just been to the post office to collect her old age pension money.
All	(*Wave excitedly*) Coo-ee!
Narrator	Look out, Mrs Green! Here comes the Brick Street mob!

(*Enter mob singing badly.*)

Mob	'Ere we go, 'ere we go, 'ere we go . . .
Narrator	Oh, no! They're after Mrs Green's old age pension money! I bet they're going to spend it on cans of coke!

(*They mug her.*)

Mob	It's the real thing! Ha-ha-ha! (*Exit laughing.*)
Narrator	Now she's got no cash for her shopping.
All	Oh, no!
Narrator	Poor old thing! Still, somebody's bound to stop and help, aren't they?
Mrs Green	Give us a hand, I've been mugged!

(*Enter a nurse hurrying.*)

Narrator	Oh, look! Here comes Nurse Goodbody from the Health Centre. She'll help Mrs Green.

Mrs Green	Give us a hand! I've been mugged!
Nurse	Sorry, dear, I've got to do a first-aid class for the Brownies. (*Exits still hurrying.*)
All	Oh, no!
Narrator	What a shame! Still, here comes Mrs Smith, the lollipop lady.

(*Enter lollipop lady.*)

	She helps the children across the road. Perhaps she'll help Mrs Green.
Mrs Green	Give us a hand! I've been mugged!
Mrs Smith	Sorry, I've got to meet my friend for coffee. (*Exits dashing.*)
All	Oh, no!
Narrator	I was sure she'd stop and help.

(*Enter headteacher rushing.*)

	Still, here comes Mrs Brown, the headteacher at the school those youngsters were from – she's bound to help!
Mrs Green	Give us a hand! I've been mugged!
Mrs Brown	Sorry, I've got to go to a parents' meeting. (*Exits still rushing.*)
All	Oh, no!
Narrator	They've all got excuses, haven't they? Nobody wants to stop and help Mrs Green.

(*Enter rollerblader.*)

All	Look out, Mrs Green!
Narrator	Here comes Gary the rollerblader – he's a grown man, he shouldn't be on the pavement! And he won't stop to help!
Mrs Green	Give us a hand! I've been mugged!
Rollerblader	Sure! I'll give you a hand up. (*Helps her up.*)
All	Well, what a surprise!
Narrator	I never expected that!
Rollerblader	Fancy some fish and chips, Mrs Green?
Mrs Green	Coo, ta! I just love fish and chips! (*They exit together.*)
Narrator	So who was the good Samaritan to Mrs Green? Was it the nurse?
All	No!
Narrator	Was it the lollipop lady?
All	No!
Narrator	Was it the headteacher?
All	No!
Narrator	Then who was it?
All	The good rollerblader!
Narrator	Would *you* have stopped to help?

Reflection

Christians believe that God wants us to share his love with everyone – not only with our family and friends. But so often we make excuses, just like the nurse and the lollipop lady and the headteacher.

Picture yourself stopping to help someone. Maybe a boy who's crying because he's fallen over or a girl who's lonely. No one else has stopped to help. But you have! It would've been easy to have made excuses like everyone else – but you've stopped to help. You're smiling because you're feeling good, and soon your new friend is smiling, too – and all because you've been a good Samaritan!

SMOKED SALMON

Bible reference
Matthew 22.1-10

Theme
The parable of the wedding feast: God's invitation to join the Church

Cast
Narrator
Mr Schofield
Mr Ramsbotham, father
Mill owner
Farmer
Mayor
Window cleaner
Lollipop lady
Painter
Caretaker
Scrap dealer
Four or more bystanders (All)

Props
Two telephones, flat cap, piece of straw to suck(!), mayor's chain of office, bucket and cloth, lollipop, paint can and brush, broom, scrap iron

It would add to the performance if the cast could try northern accents – they will be acquainted with *Coronation Street* on the television. This sketch can be played for laughs!

Narrator	Up yonder . . .
(*All hum theme from* Coronation Street.)	
	There were wedding bells in the air.
All	Ding, dong! Neeooow! (*Arms out as if flying.*)
Narrator	No, I mean Albert and Deirdre were going to get spliced!
All	A-a-a-h!
Narrator	The proud father lost no time in making the arrangements. He phoned Schofields, the caterers.
Mr Schofield	(*On phone*) Potted meat sandwiches, sir?
Father	(*On phone*) Nay, lad, smoked salmon!
All	Oh, I say! (*Very posh voices.*)
Narrator	It was going to be a real slap-up do. With live entertainment. The Brighouse and Raistrick Brass Band!
(*All hum snatch of* Edelweiss.)	
Narrator	Then Mr Ramsbotham – that was his name – sat down to write the invitations.
Father	'Ernest and Mabel Ramsbotham request the pleasure of your company at the wedding of Albert and Deirdre. RSVP.'

All	Eh? (*Scratch heads.*)
Narrator	Répondez, s'il vous plaît!
All	Eh?
Narrator	It means you've got to let them know if you're coming! Anyway, the list of really important guests was so long, he had to hire a circus tent.
All	(*Circus music*) Da-da-dadle-da-da-da-da-da-da!
Narrator	But when the invitations were delivered, Mr Ramsbotham was disappointed.
Father	Oh dear!
Narrator	The owner of the local woollen mill was too busy making . . .
Mill owner	Brass! (*Rubs hands together.*)
Narrator	I understand that 'brass' is a northern term meaning . . .
All	Money!
Narrator	And Farmer Entwhistle said he was . . .
Farmer	In the middle of harvesting.

(*All hum* The Archers' *theme.*)

Narrator	And as for the mayor, he was too busy with his racing pigeons!
Mayor	And the brass band!
Narrator	Mr Ramsbotham was brassed-off, not to say disappointed that no one could find the time to come to his son's wedding. But he decided to make other arrangements.
All	Eh?
Narrator	He went out into the street and dragged in anyone he could find. First he dragged in the window cleaner.
Window cleaner	Can I 'ave some clean water in me bucket?
Narrator	Then he dragged in the lollipop lady from the local school.
Lollipop lady	I'll have to be quick – school finishes at half-past three.
Narrator	The next person he collared was a man painting white lines in the middle of the road.
Painter	Just let me wash me brush.
Narrator	He brought in the school caretaker.
Caretaker	I've got a hundred desks to polish!
Narrator	And finally he caught the man from the local scrapyard.
Scrap dealer	Any old iron?

(*You can sing the whole song, if you like!*)

Narrator	So the party was soon full with ordinary folk like you and me. And they had a brilliant time! Can you hear them?
All	Three cheers for Albert and Deirdre! Hip, hip, hooray! (*Three times.*)
Narrator	Then Mr Ramsbotham stood up.
All	Speech! Speech!
Father	Thanks for coming!

(*All clap and cheer.*)

Father	(*Raises hand for quiet*) A toast! To Albert and Deirdre!
All	Albert and Deirdre! (*Mime raising glasses and drinking.*)

Narrator	The wedding reception had been a great success. And all because of the ordinary folk who joined in.
Father	You've made my day!
Narrator	And as for all those stuck-up people who made excuses and wouldn't come . . .
All	Don't ask them again!

Reflection

God wants everyone to come to his party! He wants everyone to belong to his church and join in with all the fun and friendship.

But some people don't want to join in. They make all sorts of excuses and try to say that they're too busy. What a shame – they're really missing out!

THE LOST GRANDCHILD

Bible reference
Luke 15.1-7

Theme
The parable of the lost sheep: Jesus searches us out at great personal cost

Cast
Narrator
Grandma
Mum and Dad
Sam
Six or more grandchildren (All)

Props
Rucksacks, chairs (to symbolize camper-van), camping gear: pan, soup mugs

The actors will have to mime wading through an ice-cold stream and climbing a steep hillside and rocks in an exhausting search. The chorus (*All*) will need to show anxiety and relief.

Narrator	There was once a grandma who had lots of grandchildren.
All	(*Waving*) Hello!
Narrator	She loved her grandchildren and wanted to get to know them better. She wanted to share a big adventure with them. So she put on her thinking-cap. She came up with a brilliant idea.
All	Yes!
Grandma	I'll take them all camping.
All	Hooray!
Narrator	So they piled her old car up with tents and sleeping-bags, and jumped in.
Mum and Dad	Goodbye!
All	Goodbye!
Narrator	And they set off for the hills.
All	(*Singing*) Here we go, here we go, here we go.
Narrator	When they got there, they pulled out the tents.
All	Heave-ho!
Narrator	And knocked in the tent pegs.
All	Bang! Bang! Bang! (*Mime*.)
Narrator	It was great up in the hills. The air was so fresh.

(*All do breathing exercises*.)

	The children were excited.
All	Yes!

Narrator	They wanted to explore, but Grandma knew that there were dangers.
Grandma	Be careful!
Narrator	She warned them to . . .
Grandma	Keep together!
Narrator	They mustn't wander off.
All	Don't get lost!
Narrator	So the children went off to explore.
All	Yippee!
Narrator	They had a wonderful time scrambling over the hillside, hiding behind bushes,
All	Boo!
Narrator	And paddling in the stream,
All	Splash!
Narrator	Grandma kept an eye on them. Soon it was time for supper.
All	Rumble, rumble, rumble. (*All hold tummies.*)
Narrator	Grandma had made the supper, and it smelled delicious!
All	Yum, yum, yum!
Narrator	But where was Sam?
All	Dunno! (*Surprise.*)
Narrator	Grandma was worried because she knew there were dangers in the hills. So she told the others to . . .
Grandma	Wait in the tent!
Narrator	She gave them a whistle to blow for help.

(*Children all whistle.*)

	Then she set off to look for Sam.
Grandma	(*Calling*) Hello-o-o!
Narrator	Grandma was used to walking in the hills but . . .
Grandma	(*Out of breath*) I'm not as young as I used to be.
Narrator	Her legs soon began to get tired. But she hunted everywhere. First, she looked down by the stream.
Grandma	Sam!
Narrator	Then she searched in the bushes.
Grandma	Sam!
Narrator	She looked behind the dry-stone walls.
Grandma	Sam!
Narrator	But there was no sign of Sam.
Grandma	Sam!
Narrator	By now, Grandma's old heart was beating fast.
All	B-boom, b-boom, b-boom.
Narrator	But she was determined to find Sam. So she scrambled up the hillside and began to climb up the rocks.
Grandma	Sam!
Narrator	There was still no sign of Sam.
Grandma	My old lungs are bursting!

Narrator	But she clambered up the hill. Then she heard a little voice . . .
Sam	Help! (*Very quiet.*)
Narrator	It was Sam. She was lost!
Sam	Help! (*A little louder.*)
Narrator	Grandma was exhausted now. But she struggled up towards Sam.
Sam	Help! (*Louder.*)
Narrator	Now she was almost there.
Sam	Help! (*Really loud.*)
Narrator	She picked Sam up! Was Sam pleased to see her?
All	Just a bit!
Sam	Grandma!
Narrator	Sam was shaking. She'd been really scared!
Sam	Grandma!
Narrator	Grandma helped Sam down the hill. The other children were waiting in the tent.
All	Three cheers for Grandma! Hip, hip, hooray. (*Three times.*)
	For she's a jolly good fellow . . . (*All join in enthusiastically.*)
Narrator	Then they all celebrated with a big mug of piping hot soup.
	Sam had got herself lost, but she'd been rescued by . . .
All	The good grandma!

Reflection

Christians believe that Jesus is a bit like that good grandma who risked her life to find her granddaughter. They sometimes call him the good Shepherd because he died for us, like a good shepherd who risks his life on the rocky hillside to save his sheep.

STORIES ABOUT JESUS

IN MY FATHER'S HOUSE

Bible reference
Mark 11.15-19

Themes
Prayer and worship; respect for people; stealing

Cast
Narrator
Jesus
Two money-changers
Six traders (All)

Props
Tables, chairs, bowls of money (*all optional*)

This sketch has a stern tone, revealing a very different aspect of the Jesus we all think we know. There needs to be a contrast between the self-seeking of the traders and the controlled anger of Jesus. Try to create a chaotic scene. If you are using puppets, then attach some simple bird and animal figures to sticks and make them dart about. If you are using actors, don't give them animal masks – it wouldn't be right in this sketch. Get the actors to mime being surrounded by escaped animals.

Narrator	Jesus strode into the Temple to pray. But what did he find?
All	Change your money here!
Changer 1	Temple coins. Best rates of exchange.
All	Change your money here!
Changer 2	Best rates of exchange!
Narrator	Jesus' face changed to thunder.
Jesus	This is my Father's house! It should be a house of prayer!
Narrator	These men, these money-changers, didn't care about God or his people. They saw only a way to be rich.
All	Buy your doves here!
Narrator	These thieving traders were selling animals for the Temple sacrifices at three times the market price.
Trader 1	Fine lambs for sale.
All	Buy your doves here. Guaranteed perfect.
Trader 2	Lambs for sale! Fine lambs for sale!
Narrator	Jesus' anger was growing.

Jesus	These men steal from the poor, and in stealing from the poor, they steal from my Father!
Narrator	Then his anger exploded.
Jesus	Out! (*Shouts, throws tables over, sets birds and animals free.*)
All	What's he doing?
Trader 3	My money! Pick it up!
Trader 4	Hey! My doves! Catch them, someone!
Jesus	Out!
Trader 5	My sheep! You can't set them free! They're mine!
Trader 6	Stop him! He can't do this!
All	Who does he think he is? He'll pay for this!
Jesus	(*Shouting*) Out! I will make this place a place of prayer where poor people can worship my Father. Not a den of thieves!
Narrator	Jesus made many enemies that day!

THE Last Supper

Bible references
Mark 14.12-52; John 13.21-30

Themes
The Lord's Supper and Jesus' arrest: friendship, betrayal, suffering, prayer, the kingship of Jesus

Cast
Narrator
Peter
John
House owner
Jesus
Andrew
Nathaniel
James
Matthew
Thomas
Judas
Four or more guards
Five more disciples

Props
Thirteen chairs (one for each disciple and one for Jesus), bread on plate, glass of red drink,
swords for guards

The scene begins in a mood of friendship and security and ends with Jesus, the Son of God, totally friendless and alone. He has been betrayed by one friend and deserted by the others. There is an atmosphere of desolation. This is the drama you will need to create in this sketch.

(*The scene is the upper room on the night of the Last Supper.*)

Narrator	What a week it had been! The triumphal entry – even if it was on a donkey! Everyone shouting.
All	Long live the King! God bless the King of Israel!
Peter	Throwing those cheats and crooks out of the Temple!
John	The time we had with Martha and Mary . . .
Peter	and Lazarus!
John	Our friends! We were like one big family,
Peter	With Jesus as the head!
John	Surely now everyone will see that he's the King!
Narrator	So they'd been sent to prepare the Passover meal – Peter and John. They'd been told to follow a man carrying a water pot. He'd lead them to a house.

	They had to say to the owner of the house,
(Enter man.)	
All	The Master sent us.
John	Where can we celebrate the Passover feast?
Man	Come with me. I'll show you.
Narrator	He'd shown them to this upstairs room. So they'd got the meal ready.
(Enter disciples and Jesus.)	
Andrew	Well, here we all are –
Nathaniel	All friends together.
James	Sharing the lamb and talking.
Narrator	But during the meal they argued about which of them was most important.
(The disciples mime arguing. Then Jesus stands up.)	
Matthew	Hold on, what's Jesus saying?
Nathaniel	He's standing up.
All	Sssh!
Jesus	This is my body, broken for you! Take, eat.
Narrator	He passed round the loaf and they each broke off a piece and ate it. But they didn't understand. Then he passed round a cup of wine.
Jesus	This is my blood, shed for you! Drink this, all of you!
Narrator	Again, they did as he said, each of them taking a sip.
Thomas	Hello, what's Judas up to?
Jesus	Go and do what you have to!
All	Something's wrong!
Andrew	He's going out into the night! *(Exit Judas.)*
Narrator	Jesus seemed very sad.
Jesus	I'm going away. But I will return! I will give you my Spirit to strengthen you!
Narrator	Then Peter, poor, blunt Peter, blurted out,
Peter	I won't let you go!
Narrator	But Jesus looked at him sadly.
Jesus	Before the cock crows, Peter, you will say three times that you never even knew me!
Narrator	Then they moved off, leaving the safety of the upper room, out into the darkness of the night, where Judas had gone before, out into the empty, echoing streets, out through the gate, out into the darkness.
All	Where are we going?
James	To the Garden – Gethsemane, you know the place!
Narrator	A happy place – but not tonight. Tonight was different! A night that was frightening, threatening, awful! In the garden, Jesus told his disciples to wait for him.
(Disciples sit down in a group.)	
	But he took Peter, James and John with him.
Jesus	My heart is breaking with sadness.
Narrator	Jesus was scared! They'd never seen him like this before. Suddenly he needed them.

Jesus	Watch with me!
Narrator	They could see the loneliness in his eyes.

(*The three disciples sit down. Jesus goes on a little way and kneels.*)

Jesus	Father, if it is possible, spare my life! But only if it is your will.
Narrator	Then what did they do? They fell asleep!

(*Disciples sleep.*)

Two times he came back to them.

(*Jesus wakes Peter, James and John.*)

Jesus	Stay awake and pray for strength. (*Jesus moves away and prays again.*)

(*Peter, James and John yawn, stretch, rub eyes, try to stay awake, but then fall asleep.*)

Narrator	But each time they fell asleep again! Jesus came back a third time.

(*Jesus wakes sleeping disciples.*)

Then it happened – the thing they'd dreaded – that tell-tale string of lighted torches!

James	Men and soldiers!
All	And Judas!
Narrator	Their wildest fears were fulfilled!
Judas	(*To guard*) The one I go up to is the man! Arrest him! (*Judas goes up to Jesus and kisses him on the cheek.*)
John	That greeting, that most poisonous of greetings!
Narrator	Then they all fled! Just when he needed them most, they were gone!
Guard	Jesus doesn't look like the King any more!
All	Just a lonely man.
Narrator	Deserted by his friends and facing who knew what!

FAITH
IN ACTION

Saint Francis and the Wolf

Theme

Caring for animals

Cast

Narrator
St Francis
Wolf
Four villagers
Six or more village children (All)

Props

None

This is a simple sketch – good for beginners. The wolf can be played by a child with a mask.

Narrator	Many years ago in Italy there was a kind and good man called Francis. He always shared what he had with poor people, but he also loved birds and animals.

(*Francis mimes stroking birds and animals.*)

	But there was one village where everyone was frightened.
	Four of the villagers went to find Francis.
All	A wolf has come down from the hills looking for food.
Villager 1	It snarls at us and we're scared!
Villager 2	No one will go to work.
Villager 3	And the children can't go out to play!
Villager 4	Please, Brother Francis, do something – we need your help!
Francis	Very well. I'll come and talk to the wolf.
Narrator	So Francis went to the village and, sure enough, the wolf came down into the streets. The people ran into their houses, leaving Francis alone in the street. The wolf saw Francis and snarled at him.

(*All snarl.*)

Narrator	But Francis didn't run away! In fact, he went up to the wolf and spoke firmly to him.
Francis	Brother Wolf, it's wrong to snarl at people and scare them! You must not do it!
Narrator	Then he bent down to stroke the wolf.

Francis	Why, Brother Wolf, you *are* thin. You must be starving! So *that's* why you came down from the hills! You've been coming down to look for food, haven't you?
Narrator	He stroked the wolf again.
Francis	If I ask the people to leave food out for you, will you promise not to snarl at them or bite them?
Narrator	The wolf seemed to nod. So Francis went off to talk to the villagers.
Francis	My friends, the poor wolf is hungry. He can't find food in the hills.
All	Then what shall we do?
Francis	The wolf has promised that if you leave food out for him, he won't harm you.
Narrator	The villagers were a bit nervous, but they began to put out food for the wolf.

(*Mime putting out food.*)

And the story goes that the wolf became gentle and played with the children.

(*All mime stroking the wolf.*)

Reflection

St Francis understood animals. He could see that when they're aggressive it's usually because they're hungry or frightened. He knew that it's best to treat wild animals with understanding and respect.

Christians believe that God has put us in charge of the world he's made. We have to take care of it. And that includes all living creatures.

PaPa PaNOV

Bible references
Matthew 2.1, 9-11; 25.31-40; Luke 2.4-7

Themes
The spirit of Christmas; seeing Jesus; helping people in need

Cast
Narrator
Papa Panov
Innkeeper
Joseph
Mary
Caspar
Melchior
Balthasar
Jesus
Dmitri
Girl
Beggar
Voice of Jesus

Props
Three gifts – gold, frankincense and myrrh, baby's shoes, stool for Papa Panov,
chair for visitors, mug, bowl and spoon, large doll in shawl

The nativity scene can be performed as a dream. At the end of the sketch, the characters reappear, again, as in a dream. We don't need to see Jesus, but we hear his voice.

Narrator	It was Christmas Eve in a small Russian village, and already it was getting dark. Papa Panov, the old village shoemaker, had finished his day's work.
All	Christmas Eve! None of the children will sleep tonight!
Papa Panov	I remember when my own children were young! But now they're grown up and far away! And my wife?
All	God bless her!
Papa Panov	She went to be with the Father long ago. And me? I shall be all alone on Christmas Day. Let's put some coffee on the stove. It's warm and cosy in my workshop. I remember I used to tell my children the story of the first Christmas.
All	Mary and Joseph came to the inn at Bethlehem . . .

(*Enter Joseph and the innkeeper.*)

Joseph	Good Innkeeper, my wife is expecting a baby. Can you let us have a room?
Innkeeper	The inn's full, sir! The only space is the cave at the back. We use it as a stable for the donkeys – there's plenty of straw.

(*Enter Mary. She sits down.*)

All	Mary had her baby there, among the animals. They were visited by the three wise men.

(Enter wise men.)

Caspar   I am Caspar. I bring a gift of gold for the new-born King.

Melchior   I am Melchior. I bring a gift of frankincense for God's Son.

Balthasar   I am Balthasar. I bring a gift of myrrh for the Saviour of the world.

(Exit Bethlehem characters.)

Papa Panov   But I have no gift for the Christ Child – or have I? Now, where did I put those shoes? Ah, here they are! It's so long since I made them. A baby's shoes, the best pair of shoes I ever made. They're fit for a new-born king! I'm so sleepy! *(He stretches and then sits down.)*

All   Time for a little snooze!

Narrator   He dreamed about Jesus.

Voice of Jesus   Papa Panov, you've been dreaming of me! Look for me tomorrow – on Christmas Day – I will visit you! But look carefully, or you may not recognize me!

Papa Panov   It was Jesus! He said he would visit me! But I've slept all night! It's Christmas morning! And he said he would come today! But will he come as a baby? Or a man – a carpenter? Or as Christ the King – God's Son? I must look out for him. I want to recognize him when he comes! *(Looks out of window.)* It's a biting cold day! Frost everywhere! Look, there's old Dmitri, the road sweeper! He looks perished! *(Going to door.)* Hey, Dmitri! You must be frozen! Come in and have a coffee to warm your old bones!

Dmitri   Thank you! It's bitter cold this Christmas morn!

Papa Panov   You look chilled to the bone, old friend!

Dmitri   This coffee is so good! I feel better already!

(Papa Panov looks out of window.)

Dmitri   Are you looking for someone?

Papa Panov   Yes, I had a dream that Jesus would come to visit me today!

Dmitri   Well, I hope he does! But I must be on my way. Thank you again for your kindness – I hope your dream comes true!

Papa Panov   Merry Christmas, old chap!

(Exit Dmitri.)

                       I must keep my eyes open for Jesus – I wouldn't want to miss him!

Narrator   Papa Panov sat at his workbench. But he couldn't concentrate. He kept stopping his work to look out of the window. The morning passed by.

Papa Panov   Time to put the soup on the stove. *(Looking out of window.)* Hello, there's someone outside – I wonder if it's Jesus? No – it's a young woman with a baby! She's so pale – and only wearing a thin shawl in this bitter weather! *(Going to door.)* My dear, come in and warm yourself by the stove.

(Enter young woman with baby.)

                       And have some soup. I'll get your baby some milk!

Girl   Thank you, sir!

Papa Panov   That's better! Why, your child has no shoes!

Girl   I've no money for shoes, sir! I'm on my way to the next village to look for work.

(Papa Panov picks up the baby shoes.)

Papa Panov	I was saving these shoes for Jesus. (*Goes to window.*)
Girl	Pardon, sir?
Papa Panov	Nothing, my dear. Your little one must have these shoes – to keep her feet warm! (*Looks out of window.*)
Girl	Thank you, sir, they're beautiful! But you keep looking out of the window. Are you expecting someone?
Papa Panov	Yes, my dear, I dreamed that Jesus would visit me today.
Girl	Then I hope he will, sir. Goodbye and thank you for your kindness!
Papa Panov	Merry Christmas. (*Takes chair to window.*)
Narrator	Papa Panov sat by the window. The afternoon passed by.
Papa Panov	Oh, dear, it's getting dark already! I *do* hope Jesus comes today! But that old beggar looks as if he's starving! There's just enough soup left to fill him a bowl! (*Calling from door.*) Let me get you some bread and soup, old chap!

(*Enter beggar.*)

Beggar	Thank you, sir!
Papa Panov	You haven't seen anyone on their way here, have you?
Beggar	Who would that be, sir?
Papa Panov	Jesus! He said he would visit me today.
Beggar	No, sir, I'm sorry! But this soup is so tasty! You're so kind, sir! Thank you!

(*They both go to the door.*)

Papa Panov	Not at all! God bless you! (*Looking up and down street.*) It's dark already! Christmas day is over. It was only a dream. Jesus never came! I'm so sleepy. (*Sits in his chair and seems to sleep.*) Hello, I can see people in the room with me!

(*As he dreams, one by one, the people he helped move forward. After speaking, each person exits.*)

Dimitri	Did you see me, Papa Panov?
Papa Panov	Who are you?
Girl	Did you see me, Papa Panov?
Papa Panov	Who are you?
Beggar	Did you see me, Papa Panov?
Papa Panov	Who are you?

(*Enter Jesus.*)

All	I was hungry and you fed me.
	I was naked and you clothed me.
	You met me today in the road sweeper, the girl with the baby and the old beggar.
	When you helped them, you helped me.
	When you were kind to them, you were kind to me.
	When you welcomed them, you welcomed me.
Papa Panov	Jesus! So you did come, after all!
All	Yes, I came to you today and I will come to you every day, in everyone you meet.

Reflection

Jesus told Papa Panov that he would come to him that Christmas day. Papa Panov was looking for Jesus, but in the wrong way. He expected to meet Jesus as he was in the Bible. But instead, he met Jesus in the road sweeper, the young woman and the beggar – all the people to whom he showed kindness. He had met Jesus without recognizing him.

Christians believe that when we are kind to someone, we are really being kind to Jesus. Will you be kind to someone today?

BABOUSHKA

Bible references
Matthew 1.1, 9-11; 6.31-33

Theme
Looking for the really important things in life

Cast
Narrator
Caspar
Melchior
Balthasar
Boy from village
Baboushka
Woman
Mary
Joseph
Innkeeper
Four or more villagers (All)

Props
Apron, brush, duster, three chairs, children's toys (in chest), table with pots, jars, three bowls and spoons (all optional, they can be mimed), bag, gifts of gold, frankincense and myrrh, large doll to represent Jesus

The first scene, in which the wise men introduce themselves, takes place on one side of the stage. Baboushka's cottage is on the other side. In the final scene, Baboushka walks several times round the stage, stopping to make enquiries on both sides – or, to make her journey even longer, she can travel around the outside of the audience in the hall before returning to the acting area for the Bethlehem scene. Her fruitless journey round the stage or the hall then continues.

(*Enter three wise men.*)

Caspar	I am Caspar, a wise man from the East. I am searching for a new-born King. We saw his star in the sky; it told us of his birth. I bring him a royal gift . . .
All	Gold.
Caspar	With me travels my learned friend . . .
All	Melchior.
Melchior	I am Melchior. I, too, bring a gift for the new-born King. My gift is. . .
All	Frankincense.
Caspar	We have searched long for this new-born King. Ah, here is our travelling-companion . . .
All	Balthasar.
Balthasar	I am Balthasar. I, too, would worship the little King. My gift for him is . . .
All	Myrrh.
Caspar	And so we come to Russia. We have travelled many miles and we still have far to go. (*He calls out.*) Boy!

(Enter boy.)

Boy	Who, me, sir?
Caspar	Yes, my son. Tell us, whose is that little cottage among the trees just down the road?
Boy	Why, sir, it belongs to old mother Baboushka. She's a funny old thing, but she makes the finest beetroot soup in the whole of Russia.
Caspar	Run down there, boy, and ask if she can give food and rest to three weary travellers.
Boy	Right away, sir. Now, won't old mother Baboushka be surprised! *(Hurries towards Baboushka's cottage.)* Three wise men – in our poor little village!
All	Mother Baboushka!
Baboushka	Not now! Not now! Can't you see I'm busy? There's work to be done. My cottage must be swept and scrubbed! *(She bustles about busily.)*
Boy	But, Mother Baboushka . . .
Baboushka	I said I was busy! There's water to be fetched from the well and washing to be done! *(Bustling about.)*
Boy	But, Mother Baboushka!
Baboushka	Then there's the cooking. I must fetch some firewood from the forest. *(Bustling about.)*
Boy	They're coming!
Baboushka	Who?
Boy	Three wise men – travellers from the East. They'll be here in a moment and they need food and rest. They want to stay in your cottage!
Baboushka	My cottage? My poor cottage? But it's in such a mess! Why didn't you warn me?
Boy	They're here now!

(Enter wise men.)

Caspar	I am Caspar! I am travelling in search of a new-born King.
Baboushka	Pleased to meet you, sir, I'm sure. What a fine gentleman! But why has he come to my poor cottage?
Melchior	I am Melchior. We are following a star in the night sky. It will lead us to a new-born King.
Baboushka	Pleased to meet you, sir. Well I never! Such fine men as these in our little village!
Balthasar	I am Balthasar. We bring special gifts for the new-born King.
Baboushka	Pleased to meet you, sir. But what can I do for you fine gentlemen?
Balthasar	Do not distress yourself. We three travel by night, following the star. But now it is day, and we need rest for our weary legs and food for our hungry stomachs.
Baboushka	In my humble cottage?
Balthasar	It is a charming home. But may we stay here?
Baboushka	Of course! Now, you gentlemen, just sit down by the fire and take the weight off your legs. I'll bring you a feast fit for kings!

(Wise men sit down.)

Narrator	So Baboushka hurried backwards and forwards, waiting on her three special guests.

(*Wise men mime eating and drinking.*)

Baboushka   Pickle, now, where did I put that pickle? (*She bustles about.*) Ah, here we are! And beetroot, they'll love this beetroot soup! Now, they must have some of my finest chutney!

(*Wise men finish eating.*)

    Now, sirs, I'll show you where you can rest awhile. Over here. (*Shows them off-stage.*) It's small but it's clean.

(*Exit wise men, each bowing his head to Baboushka.*)

    Ah, they'll soon sleep now, bless them! They must have travelled far. I know! I'll find a gift for the new-born king! The wise men can take it. I had a baby son once, but he died. It was so long ago! Now, where did I put his toys? (*Searches for toys.*) Ah, yes, here they are. But they're so dusty! They need a good wash.

Narrator   Baboushka spent the afternoon washing and drying the toys and cleaning her cottage.

(*Baboushka mimes cleaning. Enter wise men.*)

Melchior   Mother Baboushka, the sun is setting, and the stars are coming out. We must be on our way.

Baboushka   Wait, sir. I, too, have a gift for the new-born King. Please take it for me!

Melchior   I have a better idea! Why not come with us, Baboushka, and give him the gift yourself?

Baboushka   Me?

Melchior   Why not? Come quickly, Baboushka – the star is out and we must be on our way.

Baboushka   Well, I'd love to come, sir, but first I must tidy up my cottage. Wash the pots! Sweep the room! Scrub the floor! You go ahead and I'll catch you up when my house is clean.

Melchior   Thank you for your kindness, my dear Mother Baboushka. But don't forget to follow us – with your gift for the new-born King!

(*Exit wise men.*)

Baboushka   Now I must dust round this room – all these crumbs! Fancy that – three wise men! Now I must do the pots. I'll follow them as soon as I can. Now to scrub the floor. I'd love to worship the new-born King. (*Busily dusting.*) Oh, I'm so tired! I've worked all day and half the night as well. I'll just have a few moments rest. (*She sits down and falls asleep.*)

Narrator   But poor old Baboushka was so tired, she slept all night.

All   Wake up!

Baboushka   What's the time? But it's morning already! I've slept all night! I must be off or I'll never catch up with the wise men. (*Mimes quickly packing. Puts toys in bag and sets off on journey.*)

Narrator   So Baboushka set off down the road and in every village she passed, she asked,

All   Have you seen three wise men?

(*Enter woman.*)

Woman   They were here yesterday. If you hurry on down the road, you're sure to catch them up.

(*Can be repeated several times.*)

Narrator	But Baboushka never did catch up with the wise men – she had left it too late.

(Enter wise men.)

The wise men followed the star in the night sky and journeyed on to Bethlehem. There they found the new-born King, Jesus, with his mother Mary and Joseph.

(Enter Mary and Joseph.)

The wise men knelt before the baby and presented their gifts.

Caspar	I bring . . .
All	Gold.
Melchior	I bring . . .
All	Frankincense.
Balthasar	I bring . . .
All	Myrrh.

(Wise men leave. Then Mary and Joseph leave.)

Narrator	Then they left. They had worshipped the new-born King, so they set off on the long journey home. Mary and Joseph left, too, taking the baby with them, travelling to a safer place in Egypt.
Narrator	It was only then that old mother Baboushka arrived in Bethlehem.

(Enter Baboushka and innkeeper from opposite sides.)

Baboushka	Excuse me, sir, but I'm looking for a baby.
Innkeeper	You've come to the right place – there was a baby here – in the stable behind my inn. But they've gone. His parents took him away, said he was in danger – they were only just in time! But if you hurry, you'll catch them up on the road.

(Baboushka hurries on her way.)

Narrator	Old mother Baboushka hurried on down the road after Mary and Joseph and Jesus. And everywhere she went she asked,
All	Have you seen the baby king?
	Have you seen the baby King?
	Have you seen the baby king?
Narrator	But she never found him. And the sad thing is, they say she's still searching for him today.
All	Have you seen the baby King?

Reflection

What is the most important thing in life? Money? Success? Fame?

Baboushka thought it was keeping her house clean. And because she stayed to clean up her house, she missed the chance to go with the wise men and worship the Christ Child. What a shame!

So, at Christmas, and every day, ask yourself what is the most important thing in your life. Baboushka spent the rest of her life trying to catch up with the Christ Child – but she never did.

STORIES FROM AROUND THE WORLD

THE MAGIC PAINTBRUSH

Theme

Sharing

Cast

Narrator
Ma Liang
Two men
Two women
Old man
Poor man
Poor woman
Poor boy
Poor girl
Emperor
Two guards

Props

Stick, paintbrush, shape of butterfly, bowl of rice, fish, coat, axe, key

The many different scenes in this play are all suggested by the words. Props will need to appear on the stage as each is painted. This will require good organization! The hole in the ground will have to be suggested by mime. The emperor could fall behind a piece of scenery, maybe a bush. This is the only scenery needed for this play.

Narrator	Once, in China, there lived a poor boy called Ma Liang.
Narrator	Ma Liang had to work hard every day.
(*Ma Liang working.*)	
Woman 1	Ma Liang, bring those sticks!
Man 1	Ma Liang, chop the firewood!
Woman 2	Ma Liang, wash the pots!
Man 2	Ma Liang, scrub the floor!
Narrator	He loved to draw, but he was too poor to buy a paintbrush.
Ma Liang	But I can draw on the ground with this stick! (*Draws.*)
Narrator	But Ma Liang still wished he had a paintbrush.
Ma Liang	I could paint pictures for poor people!
Narrator	Suddenly an old man appeared.
(*Enter old man.*)	
	He held out a paintbrush.

Old man	Now you can paint pictures for poor people. (*Gives paintbrush to Ma Liang and exits.*)
Narrator	The old man disappeared, leaving the paintbrush in Ma Liang's hand.
Ma Liang	I can't wait to start painting!
Narrator	Ma Liang painted a butterfly. But the butterfly came to life and flew away! (*Flies away.*) It must be . . .
All	A magic paintbrush!
Narrator	Soon everyone in the village heard about Ma Liang's paintbrush.

(*Enter villagers.*)

Ma Liang	When I paint things, they come alive!
Narrator	Poor people began to ask him to paint things they needed.
Poor man	I'm so hungry! Please paint me some rice.
Ma Liang	Here, enjoy this rice.
Poor woman	Please paint me a fish.
Ma Liang	Careful, it's very slippery!
Poor boy	I'm cold! Please paint me a coat.
Ma Liang	Here, this will keep you warm.
Poor girl	I need firewood! Please paint me an axe!

(*Exit villagers. Enter emperor.*)

Narrator	Soon the story of the boy with the magic paintbrush spread across China to the royal palace. Even the emperor knew about the boy with . . .
All	The magic paintbrush!
Narrator	The emperor came to visit Ma Liang.
Emperor	Now you will paint for me!
Narrator	You see, the emperor was a very greedy man.
Emperor	Draw me a tree covered with gold coins!
Ma Liang	No! I only paint for poor people!
Narrator	The emperor was furious!
Emperor	Lock him up!

(*Guards take Ma Liang away.*)

Narrator	The guards put Ma Liang in prison.
Ma Liang	I'm so lonely!
Narrator	If only he had a key! Then he remembered . . .
All	The magic paintbrush!
Ma Liang	I'll paint a key!
Narrator	He turned the key in the lock and was soon free! (*Runs away.*)
Emperor	Catch that rascal!
Narrator	The emperor and his guards chased Ma Liang through the forest.

(*They all chase Ma Liang.*)

Ma Liang	Help! They're catching up with me!
Narrator	Then he remembered . . .
All	The magic paintbrush!
Ma Liang	What can I paint?

Narrator	Ma Liang had a brilliant idea!
Ma Liang	I'll paint a hole in the ground.
Narrator	As he painted the hole, it became real. He painted it deeper – and deeper – and deeper – and -
All	Deeper!
Narrator	Ma Liang hid behind a bush and watched as the emperor and his guards got closer – and closer – and closer – and –
All	Closer!
Emperor	H-E-L-P!
Narrator	They all fell into the hole and disappeared.

(*They go behind a screen.*)

Ma Liang	I'm safe!
Narrator	Ma Liang walked back to his village.

(*Enter villagers.*)

	He told everyone the story of . . .
All	The magic paintbrush!
Narrator	Then he went on painting things for poor people with . . .
All	The magic paintbrush!

Reflection

Ma Liang was given the magic paintbrush to help poor people. He didn't paint things for himself and he wouldn't even paint for the greedy emperor. He would only share his gift with the poor.

When we share the things we have, we make the world a happier place.

THE BELL OF ATRI

Theme
Kindness to animals

Cast
Narrator
Three citizens
Horse
General
King
Six or more citizens

Props
Bell (to be rung off stage), bell rope, creeper, horse puppet

I once performed this sketch in a school hall with a climbing-rope as the bell rope and the creeper climbing up it! If you don't have such a ready-to-hand prop, hang a rope over something high and let it dangle down. You can perhaps make a creeper from sugar paper and wire. The horse puppet can easily be made as a 'hobby-horse' by stuffing newspaper into an old sock and taping it on to a broom handle. It will have to be operated by a puppeteer.

Narrator	There was once an old bell in a tower.
All	Ding, ding, ding.
Narrator	But it hadn't been rung for years and the bell rope was frayed and falling to pieces.

(*Enter citizens.*)

Citizen 1	Look, there's a vine growing up the old bell rope.

(*They stare and point.*)

Narrator	Sure enough, a vine was twisting up and around the old bell rope.

(*Exit citizens.*)

	Now, about this time, an old general in the king's army noticed that his horse was growing old.

(*Enter general with horse puppet.*)

General	This stupid horse is useless!
Narrator	The horse had served the general well for many years. But it had grown old and tired. You'd have thought that the general would look after his horse, now it was old. But he didn't!
General	Be off with you! You're no use to me any more!
Narrator	He untied the horse and set it loose to find its own food and shelter.
General	Shoo! I'm not feeding you any more! (*Exits.*)
Narrator	The poor old horse wandered for many days with little food and at night it shivered in the cold air.
All	B-r-r-r!

Narrator	At last it came to the bell tower where the old bell was hanging. The horse saw the vine and began to nibble it.
All	M-m-m-m!
Narrator	As soon as the horse nibbled the vine, the old bell began to ring. People rushed out into the street.

(Enter citizens.)

Citizen 2	Who's ringing the bell?
Citizen 3	Look, it's an old horse! He looks hungry!
Narrator	The king came out of his palace to see what was going on.

(Enter king.)

King	Whose horse is this?
Narrator	It looks like the general's horse!
King	Then send for him at once!

(Citizens fetch general.)

Narrator	The general was called to the town square.
King	Is this your horse?
Narrator	The general was very frightened.
General	Yes, your Majesty.
Narrator	The king was angry.
King	Why have you let him loose?
Narrator	The general's knees were knocking.
General	Because he was too old for me to ride any more, your Majesty.
Narrator	The king was furious.
All	What a disgrace!
King	You should look after this poor beast! He's been a good friend to you for many years.

(Exit king with citizens.)

Narrator	And so the general took the old horse home.
All	I should think so, too!
Narrator	He looked after the horse for the rest of its life and gave it food and shelter. He learned to be kind to animals. *(General strokes horse.)* And all because of . . .
All	The bell of Atri.

Christians believe that God has made us responsible for looking after the world he has made. So it's important to be kind to all living creatures. We must care for our pets and farm animals at all times because they depend on us to look after them in return for all the love they give us.

THE BEAR

Theme
Loyalty

Cast
Narrator
Two friends
Bear

Props
None

The bear will be either a puppet or an actor wearing a mask and walking like a bear on its hind legs. A piece of very basic scenery will be required for the tree. A simple cardboard tree can be made if you have time. The actor who plays the bad friend could stand on a box behind it to give the impression of height.

Narrator	Two friends were walking through the forest one day when they heard a terrible
All	Growl!
Narrator	They stopped and looked at each other.
Friend 1	A bear! It's a bear!
Narrator	Before you could say . . .
All	Jack Robinson!
Narrator	The first man had climbed up the nearest tree, leaving his friend to face the wild beast alone.
Narrator	Now his friend knew a little bit about bears.
Friend 2	They say that a bear will not eat anyone who is dead!
Narrator	So he quickly lay down on the ground, closed his eyes and held his breath.
(*Enter bear.*)	
	The bear – a huge creature with sharp teeth and massive claws – approached the man lying on the ground, cautiously walked round him, then bent down to sniff his face. Thinking that the man was dead, he lumbered off into the forest.
(*Exit bear.*)	
	The first man climbed down from the tree and his friend got up and brushed the dust off his clothes.
Friend 1	What did he say?
Friend 2	Pardon?
Friend 1	What did he say? The bear seemed to be bending down and whispering in your ear!
Friend 2	Oh, he said, 'Be more careful who you choose for a friend!'
Friend 1	Be more careful who you choose for a friend?

Friend 2   Yes! A fine friend you turned out to be, didn't you? As soon as we heard that bear, you thought only of yourself and scampered up that tree!

(*First friend exits.*)

Are you a loyal friend? Do you stick with your friends when they're in trouble? Or do you just leave them to look after themselves? Being loyal means never letting your friends down!

THE FISHERMAN AND HIS WIFE

Theme
Being content with what you have

Cast
Narrator
Fisherman
Flounder
Wife
Three servants
Four or more villagers (All)

Props
Large pictures held up by two children to show changing backgrounds: a hut, a cottage, a castle, the sea

The seashore will be on one side of the acting area. The fisherman's house, the cottage and the castle (*all suggested by large pictures held up behind the acting area*) will all be on the other side of the acting area. The flounder can be played by a masked actor making swimming gestures or by a puppet

Narrator	A fisherman and his wife lived in a poor little hut.
(*Two children hold up picture of hut as background.*)	
All	What a mess!
Narrator	Yes, I'm afraid they didn't take much care of it.
All	It's so dirty!
Narrator	Well, one day the fisherman was on the seashore casting out his line.
(*Fisherman mimes fishing. Children hold up picture of sea.*)	
Fisherman	I've got a catch!
Narrator	He pulled in his line.
(*Flounder mimes being caught by line and pulled to shore.*)	
Fisherman	What a whopper!
Narrator	It was a huge flounder! But the fisherman had a shock – the fish spoke!
Flounder	Throw me back into the sea!
Narrator	The fisherman couldn't believe his ears!
Flounder	I'm not really a fish – I'm an enchanted prince!
Narrator	The fisherman didn't know what to say!
Flounder	I'm an enchanted prince – throw me back!
Narrator	The fisherman did as the fish asked and threw it back in the sea.
All	Splash!
Narrator	Then he trudged home.

(Fisherman walks as if very tired. Children hold up picture of hut.)

Fisherman	Wife!
Wife	What?
Fisherman	I caught a fish today – and it spoke to me!
Wife	What did it say?
Fisherman	It said it was an enchanted prince.
Wife	What did you do with it?
Fisherman	I threw it back.
Wife	Why?
Fisherman	Because it asked me to.
Wife	You've missed a golden opportunity!
Fisherman	What do you mean?
Wife	You should have asked it for a wish. Go back and say you want a wish!
Fisherman	What shall I ask for?
Wife	Ask for a pretty little cottage with a thatched roof. This is such a poor little hut.
Narrator	So the fisherman went back down to the sea and called the fish.

(Walks back. Children hold up picture of sea.)

Fisherman	Fish, fish, grant me a wish!
Narrator	The flounder came up and stared at the fisherman.
Fisherman	Flounder, I put you back in the sea, so give me a wish!
Flounder	What is your wish?
Fisherman	My wife wants a pretty little cottage with a thatched roof.
Flounder	Very well, your wish is granted!

(Fisherman walks home.)

Narrator	When the fisherman got home, his wife was standing at the door of a pretty little cottage with a thatched roof.

(Children hold up picture of cottage.)

Fisherman	Now we have everything we could possibly want!
Narrator	His wife was happy for a few weeks, but she was a greedy woman and she soon began to moan again.
Wife	This cottage is too small! We should have a castle to live in.
Fisherman	A castle? How can I get you a castle?
Wife	Go back and ask the flounder for a castle!
Narrator	So the fisherman went back to the seashore and called the fish.

(Walks back to shore. Children hold up picture of sea.)

Fisherman	Fish, fish, give me a wish!
Narrator	The fish came up and stared at him.
Fisherman	Fish, I put you back in the sea, but now my wife wants a castle to live in.
Narrator	By now the flounder was annoyed and he thrashed about angrily, stirring up big waves!
All	Splash!
Narrator	But he granted the fisherman's wish.
Flounder	Go home! Your wish has been granted!

(Fisherman walks home.)

Narrator	When the fisherman got home there was no cottage and his wife was standing outside a huge castle, ordering servants about.

(Children hold up picture of castle.)

Wife	Cook the dinner.
Servant 1	Yes, Ma'am.
Wife	Sweep the floor.
Servant 2	Yes, Ma'am.
Wife	Chop the firewood.
Servant 3	Yes, Ma'am.
Fisherman	Now we have everything we could possibly need!
Narrator	But his wife was soon moaning again.
Wife	I want to be the ruler of the world!
Fisherman	What can I do about that?
Wife	Go back to the flounder and ask him!
Narrator	The fisherman didn't want to bother the flounder again – he knew the fish would be angry – but his wife gave him no peace. So he set off for the seashore.

(Walks back to shore. Children hold up picture of sea.)

Fisherman	Fish, fish, give me a wish!
Narrator	The flounder came up and stared at him.
Fisherman	Flounder, I put you back in the sea, so let my wife be ruler of the world!
Narrator	This time the fish was really angry – thunder crashed and lightning flashed.
All	Crash!
Flounder	Go home! Your wife has what she deserves!

(Fisherman walks home.)

Narrator	When the fisherman got home, there was no castle and his wife was standing grim-faced outside their old little hut.

(Children hold up picture of hut.)

She had got what she deserved!

Isn't it sad that some people, like the fisherman's wife, are never satisfied? They want more and more and more – and why? Because they only think about themselves!

It's a pity the fisherman didn't tell his wife to be satisfied with what she'd got!

Christians believe that being envious of others and jealous of what they have makes us unhappy.

KING SOLOMON'S WISE CHOICE

Bible reference

1 Kings 3.5-28

Theme

God's gift of wisdom

Cast

Narrator
King Solomon
Two women
Guard
Four or more courtiers

Props

Large doll in shawl for baby, sword

God's voice in this sketch is spoken by the chorus (*All*). The argument between the women should be fierce.

Narrator	I knew them both! King David and King Solomon. Solomon was King David's son, you see! And I was his servant. Then, when King David died, I became King Solomon's servant. Got it?
(*Enter King Solomon.*)	
	Well, one night, in a dream, God asked King Solomon a very important question.
All	You may choose one gift, anything at all. What would you like?
Narrator	Now King Solomon knew it would be a hard job to be as good a king as King David had been.
King	I'm so young and I know so little.
Narrator	So he said,
King	I choose wisdom. Make me wise, O God!
Narrator	God was pleased with his answer and said,
All	I will make you wise.
(*Enter two women, one carrying a baby.*)	
Narrator	Well, one day two women came to him. They had a baby with them and they were arguing over whose baby it was.
Woman 1	Your Majesty, it's my baby!
Narrator	She said that they both lived in the same house and both had given birth to baby sons.

Woman 1	But *her* baby died in the night! So she took my baby and put her dead baby in bed with me!
Narrator	The other woman was angry.
Woman 2	She's lying! The baby's mine!
Narrator	King Solomon had to find out who was the baby's real mother.
All	Who is telling the truth?
Narrator	The king called his guard.
(Enter guard.)	
King	Cut the baby in two and give half to each woman.
Woman 1	No! Please don't harm him! She can have the baby!
Woman 2	Go ahead and cut the child in two!
Narrator	Then wise King Solomon knew which woman was the real mother. He smiled.
King	Give the baby to the first woman – she must be the mother because she loves him so much.
Narrator	So the woman who would rather lose the baby than see him harmed took her son home.
All	Everyone was amazed at King Solomon's wisdom.

Reflection

It's so easy to jump to wrong conclusions. Much better to take time to think things through calmly. Don't act in the heat of the moment, but think carefully about a problem and pray about it – that's the wise thing to do.

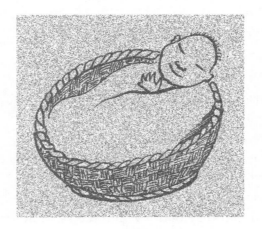

THE CLEVER RABBI

Themes
Grumbling, being content with what you've got

Cast
Narrator
Jethro
Seven friends
Rabbi
Jethro's wife and five or more children
Cock, hens and sheep

Props
None

The scenes in this play are suggested by the words. The cock, hens and sheep can be represented by children holding simple puppets. The animals will have to make a lot of noise during the scenes in the house, while the family communicate their frustration by putting their hands to their ears.

Narrator	Jethro was always moaning.

(*Enter Jethro, looking worried.*)

All	Moan! Moan! Moan!
Narrator	But what had he got to complain about?

(*Enter friends talking about Jethro.*)

Friend 1	He's got a good wife.
Friend 2	And lots of healthy children.
Friend 3	And a good job.
Friend 4	And a big house.
Friend 5	But he's always moaning.
All	Moan! Moan! Moan!
Narrator	It was true!
Friend 6	Jethro always has a long face.
Friend 7	And something to complain about.
All	Let's keep out of his way! (*Exit friends.*)
Narrator	One day Jethro was sitting in the park. The sky was blue, the sun was warm and the flowers were blooming. But . . .
All	Look at his face!
Narrator	Now Jethro was a Jew and the rabbi from the synagogue came by and saw him.

(*Enter rabbi.*)

Rabbi	Poor old Jethro! He never smiles! No one wants to go near him. He's so lonely!

Narrator	So the rabbi sat down beside him.
Rabbi	Good morning, Jethro.
Jethro	Good morning? Huh!
Rabbi	What's the matter?
Jethro	My house is too small for all my children!
Narrator	The rabbi had a brilliant idea.
Rabbi	Bring your cockerel to live in the house with you all.
Jethro	My cockerel? What good will that do?
Rabbi	Try it! (*Exits.*)
Narrator	So Jethro did! He brought the cockerel to live in the house with his family. It ran around and made a lot of noise.
All	Cock-a-doodle-doo!
Narrator (*Enter rabbi.*)	But Jethro was soon back complaining to the rabbi.
Jethro	My house is still too small!
Rabbi	Then bring the hens in.
Jethro	The hens? What good will that do?
Rabbi	Try it! (*Exits.*)
Narrator	So Jethro did! He brought the hens into the house with his family and the cockerel. They ran around and made a lot of noise.
All	Cock-a-doodle-doo! Cluck-cluck-cluck!
Narrator (*Enter rabbi.*)	But Jethro was soon back complaining to the rabbi.
Jethro	My house is still too small!
Rabbi	Then bring the sheep in.
Jethro	The sheep? What good will that do?
Rabbi	Try it! (*Exits.*)
Narrator	So he did! He brought the sheep into the house with his family and the cockerel and the hens. They ran around and made a lot of noise!
All	Cock-a-doodle-doo! Cluck-cluck-cluck! Baa-baa!
Narrator (*Enter rabbi.*)	But Jethro was soon back complaining to the rabbi.
Jethro	My house is still too small!
Narrator	But this time the rabbi said,
Rabbi	Now take all the animals outside where they used to be.
Jethro	What good will that do?
Rabbi	Try it! (*Exits.*)
Narrator (*Silence.*)	So he did, and suddenly the house was very quiet.
	And there was lots of space. Jethro dashed out to tell the rabbi.
(*Enter rabbi.*)	
Jethro	Thank you! There's plenty of space in my house now!
All	Look at Jethro – he's smiling!
Jethro	Thank you, Rabbi – you're so clever!

Poor old Jethro was not satisfied with his house. It seemed too small for all the people living there. It took the clever rabbi's trick to show him that it was really just right. Sometimes we don't see how lucky we are – until someone shows us!

Christians believe it makes us unhappy if we're always feeling envious of what other people have.

THE BASKET

Theme
Love for one another

Cast
Narrator
Boy
Father
Mother
Grandfather

Props
Big basket with straps

The basket could be a large rucksack if this sketch is being acted. Grandad does not actually have to get into it!

Narrator	Once, in a tiny village in Tibet, there lived a family. There was a little boy,
	a father,
	a mother,
	and a grandfather.

(One by one they wave to introduce themselves. The grandfather sits on a chair.)

All	But Grandfather was getting old.
Father	He can't work any more!
Narrator	All he could do now was sit at home all day.
Mother	That's all he ever does!
Narrator	Now, you'd have thought the father and mother would look after him, wouldn't you?
All	Yes!
Narrator	But they thought he was just a nuisance.
Father	He's useless!
Mother	Why should we feed him any more?
Mother	Let's get rid of him!
Narrator	So one night the father brought home a big basket.

(The father brings in a basket and puts it down. The little boy watches, goes up to the basket and looks inside.)

Father	(*To the boy*) Help me strap this on my back.
Boy	(*Puzzled*) What's it for, Dad?
Father	We'll put Grandad in here, take him up into the hills and leave him there!
Narrator	The little boy was very sad.
Boy	I'll never see Grandad again!

Narrator	The father was ready to go.
Father	Jump in, Grandad!
Boy	Dad, don't forget to bring the basket back with you!
Father	(*Puzzled*) What?
Boy	Because when *you're* old, I'll need it to get rid of *you*!
Narrator	The father stopped, thought for a moment, then put down the basket.

(*Father puts the basket down.*)

| All | He'd changed his mind. |

Reflection

The mother and father were very unloving towards the old man. Jesus said to us, 'Love your neighbour as yourself', and that includes the people in our own family! Each of us deserves to be loved and cared for because each of us is special in our own way. The little boy could see this – he just loved his grandfather.

THE KINDEST MAN YOU COULD EVER MEET

Theme
Being kind

Cast
Narrator
Robber
Junail Baghdadi
Man in street

Props
Piles of material, two big bags

This is a story from the Islamic world. The scenes and actions are suggested by the words. The old man's house and the robber's cave could be on different sides of the stage.

Narrator	There was once a cruel robber who would steal from anybody.

(*Enter robber carrying two big bags.*)

Robber	Who cares?
Narrator	One night he spotted a big house. There were no lights, so he thought . . .
Robber	There's no one in!
Narrator	He rubbed his hands together at the thought of all the loot he could steal.
Robber	Let's get cracking!
Narrator	He climbed in through an open window.

(*Mime climbing through window, and creeping into rooms.*)

He spotted some piles of rich cloth.

Robber	I'll put it in my bags.

(*Starts to pile cloth into his bags.*)

Narrator	Suddenly an old man appeared.

(*Enter Junail.*)

Robber	Where did you come from?
Junail	Can I help you?
Robber	You can help me put this cloth into my bags.

(*Junail starts to help.*)

And hurry up about it!

Narrator	When they had packed all the cloth, the burglar gave one of the bags to the old man to carry.
Robber	Quick! Let's get out of here!

(*They both mime climbing out of the window.*)

Narrator	They set off for the robber's cave, but the old man was soon tired because the bag of cloth was so heavy.

(*Junail walks slowly.*)

Robber	(*Shouting*) Hurry up! Do you want them to catch us?
Narrator	At last they reached the robber's cave. Now you'd have thought that the robber would have thanked the old man, wouldn't you?
All	Yes!
Narrator	You'd have thought he'd have shared the cloth with him, wouldn't you?
All	Yes!
Narrator	But the cruel robber just gave the old man one piece of cloth!
Robber	Now, get out!
Narrator	But the old man gave him back the cloth.
Junail	No, you keep it!
Narrator	The robber stared at him.
Junail	All this cloth is mine. Keep it!
Narrator	The robber still didn't understand what the old man meant.
Junail	It was my house you burgled!
Narrator	The robber couldn't believe his ears!
Junail	You must be very poor if you wanted to steal my things, so I decided to help you. (*Exits.*)
All	The robber didn't know what to do.
Robber	I've never known such kindness!
Narrator	He walked back to the old man's house and stopped someone in the street.

(*Enter man.*)

Robber	Who lives in this house?
Man	Junail Baghdadi – he's the kindest man you could wish to meet!
Narrator	The robber knocked at the door.

(*Mime knocking. Enter Junail.*)

Narrator	The robber knelt down in front of the old man.
Robber	Please forgive me!
Junail	Of course, my friend!
Narrator	And he never stole anything again, but worked hard and lived . . .
All	An honest life.

Reflection

The old man was so kind that the robber decided to change and never robbed anyone again. It was a turning point in his life – and all due to the old man's kindness.

Perhaps today we shall have a chance to be kind. Perhaps our kindness will change someone's life. Picture yourself being kind – maybe to someone who has been unkind to you. Your kindness might make all the difference. It might give that person new hope or a new start.

Jesus knew that showing friendship can change lives – the story of Zacchaeus the tax collector illustrates this.

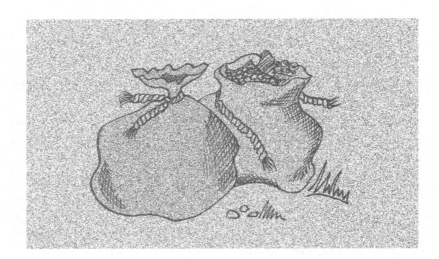

Also available:

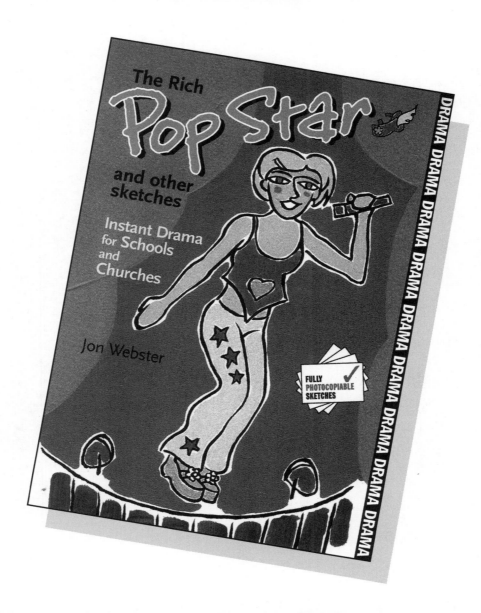

Same author. Same style. Different content.
If you liked one, you'll like the other.
Simple really.